Malcolm McCulloch Paterson

Compensation discharge in the rivers and streams of the

West Riding

Malcolm McCulloch Paterson

Compensation discharge in the rivers and streams of the West Riding

ISBN/EAN: 9783337374488

Printed in Europe, USA, Canada, Australia, Japan

Cover: Foto ©Andreas Hilbeck / pixelio.de

More available books at **www.hansebooks.com**

COMPENSATION DISCHARGE

IN THE

RIVERS AND STREAMS

OF THE

WEST RIDING.

BY

MALCOLM McCULLOCH PATERSON, M. INST. C.E.

London:

E. & F. N. SPON, 125, STRAND.

New York:

SPON & CHAMBERLAIN, 12, CORTLANDT STREET.

1896.

PRICE TWO SHILLINGS.

COMPENSATION DISCHARGE

IN THE

RIVERS AND STREAMS

OF THE

WEST RIDING.

BY

MALCOLM MCCULLOCH PATERSON, M. INST. C.E.

London :

E. & F. N. SPON, 125, STRAND.

New York :

SPON & CHAMBERLAIN, 12, CORTLANDT STREET.

1896.

COMPENSATION DISCHARGE

IN THE

RIVERS AND STREAMS

OF THE WEST RIDING.

————◆•◆•◆—— ——

I.

A NEGLECTED BRANCH OF RIVER CONSERVANCY.

The West Riding Rivers Board was constituted in 1894. The writer set forth at the time their special powers, at the same time expressing his view that they did not by any means cover the whole ground. The Act is truly the Charter of the rivers of the West Riding. It created an influential body whose sole interest was the protection of the rivers from their sources to the confines of the Riding. But its limits are narrow, and the powers it confers are restricted. The Board's self-imposed task is one of extraordinary difficulty, and no experienced observer can doubt that to succeed in it, new and wider limits and powers must be secured. Happily, even two short years of public discussion and action have brought public opinion—that indispensable factor in all legislation—more into accord with scientific judgment.

In view of the arduous nature of their task, public curiosity keenly watches the conflict of this Board and of the Mersey and Irwell Committee, with the forces of pollution. Perhaps the latter is the more interesting problem, for the pollutions of the West Riding, terrible as they are, are not focussed into a huge and practically stagnant canal. But it is not intended here to make any detailed survey of the progress made. In fact, the

4

results *in esse* are not great, whatever may be the results *in posse*. Like a lion in the path, the formidable question of the trade effluents faces us, and all are convinced that until some practical solution of this problem is found, the Aire and Calder will not be perceptibly improved.

One method of hastening the result or solving doubts does, indeed, suggest itself to those behind the scenes. Many authorities, whose sewage works are already in operation, have designed those works and sewers to be used by manufacturers for the discharge of their effluents under certain reasonable conditions ; but there being no pressure, the manufacturers in these districts do not so use them. All that is needed, it is thought, is a notice from the Rivers Board to such offenders to cease the fouling of the streams which still goes on, yearly increasing. Then when the trade refuse of any district is collected into the sewers, and the whole volume of combined sewage is fully treated, the difficult problem as to whether or not the refractory combination of domestic sewage and woollen trade refuse can be successfully dealt with, may be near its solution. Once satisfy authority on this point, and the way is open. To see clearly what can and what cannot be done is the first step to reform. Naturally, therefore, great cities like Leeds and Bradford, not seeing clearly, hesitate to adopt the provisions of the 7th clause of the Rivers Pollution Act, 1876, and to offer to all their manufacturers the use of their sewers for their innumerable foul effluents, no matter how great their contributions may be to the drainage rate. Nevertheless, Leeds has within the last few weeks taken a most important step in this direction, by offering to admit the effluents of the tanneries and leather-trades to the sewers, conditionally upon the provision of proper settling tanks for the grosser solids.

At a recent meeting, the Chairman of the West Riding Rivers Board, Mr. Milnes Gaskell, who has the highest sense of the claims of the rivers upon the district whose vast wealth they have helped to create, made a strong and fitting pronouncement on the situation. Conscious of the methods of many authorities, who, as a matter of simple fact, will do nothing more than they are forced to do, and lag behind from stage to stage, viewing all new drainage as a superfluity, he said " he felt that the days of moral suasion were drawing to an end, and that this year would see the exercise of the powers conferred upon the Board by the Act of 1894 to overcome the breaches of many offenders, and the shameful misuse of the rivers and streams of the West Riding." Thus tact and policy have their limits. They have well fulfilled their purpose in conciliating the public, and in fostering, if not creating, a new ethical sense—that of reparation to those same rivers and streams ; but, after all, they are but as the soft prelude to a vigorous drama.

Coming to the real subject-matter of this article, it is desired to draw special attention to the action of the West Riding County Council with respect to the discharge of compensation waters into the rivers of their district. This action, so far as we know, has not been followed by any other county council. Therefore, inasmuch as all pioneers against abuses of long standing suffer from the ignorance, not so much of their direct opponents, who are merely guided by their personal interests, but of outsiders who are impatient of any new thing they cannot understand ; it seems to us that the case is essentially one whose merits must be driven home to all concerned. And we think it can be demonstrated that every community is concerned whose river sources are impounded and used for the service of man.

Curiously enough, the important principles which should govern the discharge of such compensation waters have been completely lost sight of down to a very recent period. Yet they vitally affect the *régime* of the compensated rivers, and will, it may safely be said, increasingly demand the jealous consideration of all conservancy boards. Now let us see the genesis of this important forward step of the West Riding County Council.

In 1888, after the abnormal drought of 1887—the Jubilee drought—Halifax sought to extend its water supply. Amongst its opponents was Sir John (now Lord) Savile, who petitioned against the principle adopted in the Bill of discharging compensation waters intermittently ; that is to say, for twelve hours a day only, and for six days in the week. Sir John Savile and his advisers had a large experience of compensation waters, and for nearly thirty years had seen the catchment areas of his extensive moorland properties at the head waters of the Calder appropriated for the wants of the great trading communities below. Time after time Halifax and Wakefield had come to Parliament asking for more of the pure water they yielded, and had got it. At first, the effect of the intermittent method of compensation flow was not noticed. But, as the schemes came into operation, light was thrown upon the subject, and it was found that, in the opinion of Sir John's agent, a most serious injury had been unwittingly inflicted upon the estate by Parliamentary sanction and with the consent of all concerned.

This disastrous result, as might be expected, was soon driven home by the years of drought, and when in 1888, after the "Jubilee" drought, Halifax was forced once more to come to Parliament for powers to construct further works on Sir John Savile's estate, the latter was found amongst the petitioners against the Bill, opposing those clauses which provided for the discharge of the compensation water by an intermittent flow. The opposition failed in the Commons Committee, notwithstanding very plain evidence of the damage, not only to the lower section of the moorland stream impounded, but to the River Calder below. It was shown that the Walshaw Beck--at Hardcastle Crags, one of the most romantic scenes in a romantic district---would continue to be, as it had been, a beautiful stream by day, and a dry ditch by night and on Saturdays and Sundays. That the millowners 10 or 12 hours down the river, if we measure time by the usual current flow, would lose the compensation waters, which would pass their wheels at night ; and that the alternate ebb and flow of the river once a day would be a serious sanitary injury in any polluted stream. All this notwithstanding, the thing was new, while the so-called paramount millowner's interest was old, and the latter prevailed.

In the Lords' Committee a still stronger effort was made. Overwhelming evidence from the lower millowners was adduced in favour of a continuous natural flow, while not a single millowner appeared against it. The promoters declared that they were entirely indifferent in the matter, and the town clerk said that the stream, which is a favourite resort of the Halifax people, ought not to be permitted to be entirely dried up on Saturdays and Sundays, if it could be helped. It could be helped ; and the Lords' Committee, in probably the very first Parliamentary fight on this phase of the question, substituted a continuous flow for the intermittent flow proposed. Thus an innovation was made, and a precedent within the Riding created, wherein other interests than merely those of water-power millowners or water carriage owners were consulted.

In that year, 1888, county councils were by law established. Two years later, Bradford applied to Parliament for its great water works extension in the Nidd Valley. This was something entirely new to that sequestered dale, and the land-owners having no knowledge of the true meaning of intermittent compensation, judgment would certainly have gone by default, and like owners on other compensated streams, they would have awakened too late to find their river deprived of its birthright of a natural continuous flow, had not the new authority stepped in, and in the common interest, and upon public grounds alone, secured a continuous flow. The entry of the County Council upon the scene was caused by a fortuitous circumstance, which speaks for itself. In that same year, 1890; Morley was pursuing its water scheme in Parliament. Here again the interests of Lord Savile were attacked, and the promoters were threatened with opposition if they did not grant a continuous flow. In this action, Lord Savile's interests were represented by Mr. Wm. Lipscomb, his agent, who has, in fact, pioneered this important movement.

While this threat was hanging over them, an inquiry was held in the district by three members of the County Council, before whom it was given in evidence that the state of the River Calder at Mytholmroyd was so bad that it was the principal cause of the sickness then and there prevalent; and that the tributary which Morley was at that moment seeking to impound, was the last pure stream of any magnitude which entered the river above Mytholmroyd. Upon this hint the County Council took action, and, as a result of the joint representations of Lord Savile, the County Council, and the Calder and Hebble Navigation, the Morley Corporation gave way, and adopted the principle of a continuous flow.

Thus brought face to face with this hitherto obscure branch of rivers conservancy, the County Council speedily grasped its true importance, and wisely determined to secure in all future water schemes within their district the continuous natural flow of all waters dedicated as compensation to rivers for waters abstracted.

In the Nidd case, the usual argument as to the paramount interests of water power was used, but here, again, as in the Halifax Bill, millowners were found to come forward and declare the injury that would accrue to them if an intermittent flow were enacted.

It may serve to show how little attention has been given to the flow of water in river beds, if we record that, in this case, the most important riparian witness in favour of a continuous flow had already agreed to the original proposal for an intermittent flow. He had given little thought to the matter, but possessed a vague impression that water discharged over the compensation gauge at Gouthwaite—a distance of 10½ miles—at 6 A.M., would reach his wheel before breakfast. His views experienced a revolution when his own miller told him that in ordinary dry weather the swell of the tail water from the next mill above—a distance of but five miles—was not perceptible in less than four hours. Taking stoppages into account, about one mile to one and a quarter miles an hour is the usual ordinary dry weather velocity in these impounded Yorkshire streams.

Evidence was also given from a sanitary point of view, and as touching the beauty of the river and its fishing interests. The scheme was a great one, the greatest ever promoted in Yorkshire, and much depended on the issue. Fortunately, in the chairman of the Commons Committee (the Council were too late for action in the Lords) the public had the very best guarantee that all the interests of the river would be considered. Mr. James Stansfield, M.P., had sat for Halifax for a whole generation, and the whole county of York could not have furnished a man who, from actual personal knowledge, could bring to bear on the question a riper experience of the evils wrought upon the industrial rivers of the West Riding by the countless abuses they suffered, amongst which not the least was this daily practice of drying up and re-filling the river beds.

After three witnesses had been heard, the Committee stopped the evidence, and announced their intention of granting a continuous flow, which was ultimately fixed at not less than 5,000,000 gallons daily. This was a long step forward, but the Chairman and his Committee did not stop here. On their representation a new order was introduced into the Standing

Orders of both Houses, which runs as follows : " In the case of every Bill whereby it is proposed to impound the whole or any part of the water of any river or stream, and to give a flow of water in compensation for the water so impounded, the Committee on the Bill shall inquire into the expediency of making provision, so far as may be practicable, that the whole or a minimum amount of such compensation water shall be given in a continuous flow throughout the twenty-four hours of every day." (110th Standing Order, House of Lords.)

In 1892 the Leeds and Liverpool Canal Company applied for the power to impound and divert the waters of the best remaining feeder to the Aire. A novelty in the application was that the company, apparently sure of its ground of prescriptive right, had actually built the largest of its three impounding reservoirs before its application was made to Parliament, and had the application failed, the reservoir would have been useless. The prescriptive right was that of impounding as much water as they needed for the purposes of navigation from every important feeder of the Aire, including this one—the Winterburn Beck—from its source to Leeds, except two. This right was conferred by their Act of 1769, at a time when the population of the valley of the Aire was not more than 100,000. Now the population is 900,000, and the effect of this wholesale interception of nearly all the pure water above Keighley by the canal, and of nearly all below it by Bradford, Keighley, Shipley, and other places, is probably without a parallel in this country, except in the Calder basin. In dry weather the canal flows in limpid reaches bearing the water belonging to the river, which, on the other hand, stagnates in fetid black pools, filling the air with a sickening stench. Brindley and the original promoters of this important water-way did not foresee so calamitous a result, nor did the Parliament which sanctioned it ; but there it was, and there it would have remained but for two things, viz : this application of 1892, and the existence of a county council. The Bill of the promoters, it is true, provided compensation, but it was a parliamentary compensation only, not a real one ; for in dry weather every drop of it, being discharged above the existing intake weirs of the company, was to be trapped by them, and so conveyed, not into the River Aire, to which for 117 years it had been due, but into the canal itself. No millowners opposed this astonishing proposal, for there were none within the 20 miles from the lowest reservoir, prescribed by standing orders as the limit of notice to millowners. But the County Council intervened, and secured to the river a continuous flow, which already has proved of great benefit to the riparians, sanitarily and otherwise.

We now come to what has been the water fight of the last two sessions—two, because of the suspension of the Barnsley Bill caused by the dissolution of 1895. This was the struggle for the last unappropriated feeder of the Don, known as the Little Don. The contest was originally triangular, between Dewsbury, Barnsley and Sheffield. Each of the two former wanted a separate and distinct section of the catch-ground, neither interfering with the other; while Sheffield, with whom were allied Doncaster and Rotherham, wished the whole basin of the Little Don to be reserved for their own future wants. The latter had no Bill for appropriation, but were leagued in opposition to the schemes of Dewsbury and Barnsley.

The merits of this interesting struggle form no part of our present purpose, but it is necessary to state that in the present session Sheffield appeared as a promoter of a Bill of its own, to appropriate the whole catch-ground for the uses of itself, Doncaster, and Rotherham, with the privilege to Barnsley of buying a supply of water to the extent of $1\frac{1}{2}$ millions of gallons per day at arbitration price. Dewsbury, which had conceded the continuous flow, saw its application summarily thrown out last year on grounds entirely distinct from the needs of the opposing parties. Barnsley proposed an intermittent flow, and so did Sheffield. The real promoters of that form of discharge were the millowners of the River Don—probably the most compact and powerful body of millowners in this country; and it is this body which, throughout this protracted conflict, have been the opponents of the County Council. As in the previous Bills cited, Barnsley did not care how the compensation was discharged but Sheffield, on the other hand, somewhat sided with the Don millowners, not having as yet realized the true signification of intermittent flow.

What took place in Committee upon the Barnsley and Sheffield Bills is the proximate cause of this attempt to lay down an outline of the principles which should govern the discharge of compensation water. Committees of either House do not, as a rule, care to distinguish themselves by taking a course athwart what seems the general tide of popular opinion ; neither are they to be expected to discern at once the turning point in that tide, nor to realize what so experienced a West Riding member as Mr. Stansfield saw at once, namely, the far-reaching evils of the insidious form of rivers pollution we treat of—intermittent compensation—nor, it may be added, the defects of the machinery controlling that compensation. Consequently what seemed perfectly clear to a judgment ripened under a life-long experience of river beds, or rather, sewer beds, as they may more fitly be termed, alternately wet and dry daily, did not seem so clear to minds to which the whole question was new ; and it is to be feared that committees at the close of a protracted inquiry have not always that patience without which we cannot learn. No apology therefore is needed for throwing light upon the whole question of the discharge and administration of rivers compensation.

Barnsley passed its Bill through the Lords last year ; the Committee, with the Earl of Jersey as its Chairman, rejected the plea of the County Council for the substitution of a continuous for an intermittent flow of compensation water. This part of the Bill was relegated to the close, being heard on the clauses. Human life has its parallel in that of Committees. In their youth, time is of no value ; they spend it prodigally in trifles, and when age comes on they have none to spare. The policy of calling strong local evidence first, to rivet the wandering attention of the members, was not followed. Riparians whose interests had to suffer or profit for ever from the Committee's decision, and who were prepared to give their reasons for a continuous flow, and for an independent control, stood aside, giving place to experts and others who merely spoke on the general question. Possibly this omission may have had its influence on the result ; be that as it may, the millowners gained the day.

The step taken by Sheffield in depositing a Bill to appropriate the whole catch-ground, determined the destiny of the Little Don compensation water. In the Barnsley case the volume dealt with was comparatively small; the importance of the principle was not appreciated by those millowners most nearly concerned. But when it was seen that the last unappropriated feeder of the River Don above Sheffield was to be absorbed, at a single mouthful, as it were, the attention of all concerned was focussed upon the question. For the first time men saw clearly, and this being accomplished, it was an easy matter to break through the chains of long association. Hence the millowners, hitherto united and impregnable, became a divided body, and the longer the subject was considered, the more certain grew the result. Let us see how the case stood.

Above the city of Sheffield, which sends down its sewage in a continuous daily flood of nearly 10,000,000 gallons, the River Don has a catchground of 66,000 acres. This is the area at the junction of the Loxley. Of this area no less than 26,750 acres were already appropriated by the towns of Sheffield, Dewsbury, and Barnsley, such appropriation including the entire available area of three out of the four great feeders, namely, the Don proper, the Ewden (at present not utilised), and the Loxley. The one remaining area—that of the Little Don—contains 8750 acres of available catch-ground, and this was now to be taken. Thus, out of a total of 66,000 acres, no less than 35,500 acres would be absorbed if the scheme passed; and it may be safely estimated that this 35,500 acres, with much greater rainfall, and much less absorption and evaporation, would acre for acre, yield to the stream more than double the volume yielded by the remaining 30,500 acres below, and that volume of a far purer character.

Coming to the millowners' point of view, what makes their position look strange is the fact that the whole of the twenty odd mills from Langsett, on the Little Don, down to below Sheffield, run day and night, mostly for 21 hours daily, and in at least one case—that of a paper mill—24 hours. Yet up to the application of the Sheffield Corporation for the Little Don, a 12 hours' flow of compensation was the almost universal rule, the following being the exact volumes:

Day Flow.

		Gallons per Day.
Sheffield Water Works (existing)	...	9,113,472
,, ,, (appropriated)		2,683,281
		11,796,753
Dewsbury ,,		2,018,000
Barnsley ,,		810,000
Total	... ...	14,624,753

Night Flow.

Dewsbury	... ...	300,000

By the new scheme this vast disproportion was to be still further increased by adding to the day flow the entire compensation from the Little Don—5,300,000 gallons per day—making in round numbers a 20 million gallons day flow and a 300,000 gallons night flow. This was for a river whose mills all run, more or less, day and night! But, it may be suggested, what of the ordinary dry weather flow of the lower sections of the river and its affluents below the catch-grounds? To which the answer is, that the 30,500 acres of these lower lands would for a considerable period in each year yield no more than $\frac{1}{4}$ cubic foot per second per 1000 acres, or about 2½ millions for 12 hours, making, with the handful from Dewsbury, a total night flow from all sources of about 2¾ million gallons, as compared with a total day flow of 22¼ million gallons. As soon as the upper millowners had fairly grasped these facts, they realised the disaster which would ensue; to wit, the loss of at least one-half of the entire compensation water from this last feeder. In these mills the proportionate loss would be greatest, their fall being greater and their volume being less than lower down; and after the figures had been fairly placed before them, important millowners were prepared to come forward and testify that the intermittent flow would be disastrous to them, and that in some cases they would not only lose the power required at night, but that their wheels could not profitably utilise the whole of the day flow if thus doubled by intermittent discharge.

Thus divided in their ranks, the millowners looked carefully into a matter to which probably they had never before given any serious attention, and upon which they had acquired no accurate knowledge ; after which they wisely yielded without putting the County Council to the trouble of proving their case in Committee. A compromise was agreed upon, whereby the River Don received a night flow of 2,000,000 gallons. The exact volume under an *equal* continuous flow would have been 2,271,428 gallons, so that this timely opposition secured about seven-eighths of the required volume. The greatest loss was in the volume allotted for the Sunday flow, only 1,800,000 gallons being secured for the whole 24 hours, instead of 5,300,000 gallons—a difference which would have been worth fighting for before a strong Committee. Sunday, is of all days that upon which a stream, especially if it be, as is the case with the Don and all its upper feeders, a beautiful stream, and its banks the favourite resort of a vast public, should be the most wholesome and pleasing to the senses —a recreation to both body and mind—while even from a utilitarian point of view, a cessation of flow on Sunday means the stoppage of mill wheels on Monday below a certain point. Nevertheless, while not complete, the victory was substantial. The principle of a continuous flow, though not of an *equal* continuous flow, which is the true principle, was maintained, and for the first time in the history of the Riding this principle received the sanction of the representatives of the whole mill-owning body.

In the matter of control the County Council were less fortunate. This issue was fought out to the last. As already hinted, in private Bill legislation a strong Committee is needed to set aside old precedents and to set up new ones, asserting the public good, and overruling that timorous legislation which is based on custom only. The Council, from the very onset, felt that in pursuing the principle that *all* the interests of the rivers should be considered in the treatment of compensation water, one thing was imperative ; to wit, the representation of *all* such interests in that authority upon which the duty would devolve of enforcing those provisions they had succeeded in securing after such strenuous efforts. The same principle was common to both. It may be thought that this principle should be evident to any legislator as a plain, even an axiomatic, principle of justice in all legislation. So thought the County Council, but they reckoned without their host.

They asked that the power of enforcing the penal clauses relating to the discharge of compensation water should be placed, not with the millowners, as provided by the Act, but with themselves, and also with the West Riding Rivers Board. Two controlling authorities may be thought superfluous ; but the title of the West Riding County Council, or the West Riding Rivers Board, as the representative of *all* interests, to see the law administered, is indefeasible. The education of public opinion is, however, necessarily slow. The Committee received both the plea and the evidence coldly, and after a short and unsatisfactory hearing abruptly announced their decision in favour of the millowners, who will, therefore, have the pleasing duty of recovering and distributing the penalties provided in the Act for, amongst other things, any omission to discharge on Sundays that very compensation volume which they did their best to keep out of the Bill. This decision was given in the teeth of direct evidence, which was not even questioned, that undertakers of waterworks have actually themselves become the millowners. In conclusion we have in the Committee's decision the proof that there is a deep-rooted conviction that a stream exists only for the millowners.

The fact of this extraordinary decision, together with that of the Lords' Committee last year against that same principle of continuous flow assented to by the millowners themselves this year, demands a more full and exact knowledge of the issues at stake, than has yet been grasped by the body politic. It has been thought well, therefore, to devote the following pages to setting forth those principles which appear to be involved in the discharge and control of compensation waters to streams. It is an undoubted fact that most water works engineers themselves, while expert in every method of assessing compensation volumes, rarely trouble themselves with their application, and are but seldom called upon to act at once as the advising engineer both for the impounders and the conservators of any stream ; a position which has the advantage of enabling a man to see both sides of a not very difficult question.

II.

CONTINUOUS v. INTERMITTENT COMPENSATION IN RIVERS.

In the treatment of every industrial stream in the West Riding, and, it may be added, everywhere else, we find pollution in two distinct categories. There is pollution positive and pollution negative. Pollution positive everybody knows; pollution negative was practically unknown a few years ago, though it has existed for ages; and even now, few, indeed, are aware of its existence.

Briefly, positive pollution may be defined as the addition of solid or liquid filth to a stream of naturally clear water; while negative pollution is abstraction of any portion of that naturally clear water from any stream which has received, or may receive further down, positive pollution.

If a community discharge its sewage, a manufacturer his foul effluents, or any person casts into a stream the carcase or offal of a sheep, dog, or cat, the effect is seen and felt. But if some person quietly reduces the volume of pure water at its fountain head, the sufferer below is mostly unconscious of the injury. Sanitarily, a casuist might say, with Iago, that the river that is robbed, no person knowing that it is robbed, is not robbed at all. But, though the cause is unseen and unknown, the effect is both seen and known, and the very mystery of its true origin makes the danger more insidious.

Every water analysis is merely a question of proportion. So much water—so much free ammonia, so much albumenoid ammonia, so much lime, so much common salt, and so forth; and if the proportion falls below a certain standard, the water is pronounced pure. If it were worth while, therefore, one could make dirty water clean, without filtration, by dilution; merely, that is, by pouring into it a certain volume of the pure element. That, of course, we cannot do upon a practical scale, nor would it be worth while if we could. But we can render more or less tolerable, or intolerable, the pollution of a stream by the dilution of its dirty vapid waters with a certain volume of pure and cold water. This brings us to river compensation.

What is compensation as applied to rivers? The attention given by our busy profession to the theory of this most important question may be gauged by the fact that there is no treatise extant upon it, so far as the writer and others have been able to discover; no book, nor even any pamphlet, however modest. In every adequate water works treatise, the subject is touched upon, but merely as an incident, in which the principles governing the assessment, significance, duty, and discharge of compensation water are absolutely passed over. True, the *mode* of assessment is given, but the principle remains untouched. Even the calculations upon which a certain volume is assessed as a fair compensation for water to be taken, which calculations should be based on adequate gaugings of the stream in relation to rainfall, are rarely made for this purpose. No doubt, in the infancy of compensation to rivers, these facts were more regularly observed, in a fashion, inasmuch as at the outset some basis of assessment could not be dispensed with. But now custom rules, and the average rainfall being determined approximately, the volume available by the impounding works is settled by comparison with other districts; and of the available volume it is at present the rule to dedicate one-third to the stream and two-thirds to the impounding authority.

The settlement of the available volume is a contest in which rival engineers and meteorologists are the chief actors; the one side trying to secure for the millowners as much, and the other trying to get off with as little, as they can. Generally, substantial justice is done, especially where, as in the millstone grit formation, so wide an experience of actual measured results has been obtained. But in other geological formations, where the rainfall, evaporation, and percolation are less known, grave mistakes have been made, generally in favour of the stream, so far as the aggregate flow is concerned, and water authorities have found themselves crippled by a load of compensation water beyond the capacity of their works.

In such cases, without repeated experience to guide them, it becomes the duty of the promoters to proceed with caution. Time and careful observation only can render their position safe.

Geological structure, dislocation, contour and slope, cultivation, and even the bearing of slopes in relation to the winds which sweep in the rain-clouds, have each an influence on evaporation and percolation, and may disturb any hypothetical conclusions derived from different conditions. Most mistakes in this matter have been due, as most mistakes are, to excessive haste. There has been no time to put down gauges and to record, year after year, the daily rainfall as compared with the actual daily stream flow from the catchground. Putting off the evil day of a further large expenditure of capital, from which, as a rule, no return can be expected for years, the promoters wait until a prolonged drought makes immediate action necessary. Then they say, in effect, "Time presses, and all must be left to fortune ; we have no leisure for detailed observations ; " and so no gaugings are taken, nor, as a consequence, any means obtained for determining certain facts of importance, as for instance :

a. The fitness of any waterwheel for its supposed duty ; that is, its proportion to the volume of river water available.

b. The average number of working days in the year on which any mill concerned can work, all stoppages from excess of water in floods, and defect of water in drought, being deducted.

c. The true value of the water power of each mill concerned, and also of each stream whose sources are to be impounded.

It is certain that these observations would bring out the fact that the value of water power on uncompensated mountain streams has been systematically over-estimated. We have known a case where a fine turbine has been erected, nominally yielding 40 horse-power for night and day use, whereas to furnish such a power the whole year round, the entire available rainfall from the catchground above the wheel would have been required, at a probable cost in reservoir space of half a million sterling. But the observations are rarely made, and so water power remains overrated, while every other interest in the stream remains underrated.

The promoters of every system of gravitation water works—by which it will suffice here to understand every system of water supply dependent upon the impounding and storage of water which has arrived at some definite natural channel by its own unaided gravitation— are then bound in this country to give out to the stream below, a certain daily compensation flow. One-third of the total available volume may be too much, but is rarely, we may even say never, too little. Such a volume meted out daily, acts as a regulator usually far exceeding in value the whole available volume of the stream in its natural state. The maximum flow of a stream is sometimes as much as 600 or 800 times its absolute minimum dry weather flow. These fluctuations are reduced by storage, and the nearer the impounding works the greater the benefit to all the interests. This being so, how comes it that compensation waters, instead of being a blessing from a sanitary point of view, are mostly, in the West Riding of Yorkshire, a curse? The answer is clearly; because, while the natural stream, fluctuate as it may, comes night and day, week-day and Sunday alike, the compensation flow on nearly the whole of the industrial rivers comes intermittently.

All these rivers have been full of beauty and interest, teeming with fish and haunted by wild fowl. They wind through rich pastures and cornfields and romantic dales and woodlands. The imagination may depict their metamorphosis into a pestilential solitude ; the silent passing of the clear rivers, the children of the mountain mist, into fetid sewers. The owner far down the doomed stream asks himself the question, " Here is the dirty water ; where is the clean water gone ? " Is there no kind of dilution ? His family sicken, so do his cattle ; and so, also, do the aquatic plants that abounded by the river bank, giving place to noisome weeds. At length his river-side house—the house of his fathers—becomes to him uninhabitable, and he leaves it for health's sake. He has no redress; his interest is not recognised; and hitherto he has had no one to assert it.

Between them, the engineer and manufacturer have effected the change. The engineer has, as he is wont to boast, converted this force of nature, pure water, to the uses of man at the higher, and the millowner has done it at the lower, levels. The purest water is laid hold of and imprisoned in reservoirs and pipes, passed through sinks of every conceivable form, human and otherwise ; collected in drains, and then discharged, more or less foul, into the river. The manufacturer does the same in another fashion with the next purest water, and the metamorphosis is complete. The Latin poet could invent no transformation more strange ; the force of change can go no further. The only alleviation is dilution, in which the compensation flow should play its part. So it does, but in a manner so opposed to nature that the river would often be better without it.

Our landowner down the river has observed a phenomenon in its defiled current. It has not only become an open sewer, but it ebbs and flows once a day, and both ebb and flood occur within a very brief space of time. The river remains at a higher or a lower level for 10 or 11 hours together. The lower level obtains during the whole of the morning, after which, perhaps, an hour or so after noon, the current swells silently and soon covers, long before they are dry, the foreshores of black fetid mud which before were visible. Late at night again, if necessity or ill-fortune have brought him back to the river side, he may discern, not by the sight, for it is dark, but from the increasing stench which salutes his nostrils, an ebb as silent and swift as the morning flow, disclosing once more those same foreshores, with the addition of a new film of that fetid black mud of which they are largely composed. What was a beautiful river at one time is now not unlike a dry ditch or sewer. The murmur of running water over the shingle is hushed, and Nature seems to have taken her final leave. He witnesses the combined result of positive and negative pollution : the sweet, pure, and cold water which formerly fed the stream has gone entirely, two-thirds of it being converted into town sewage, and the remaining third sent down intermittently.

Further, he finds that the ebb continues over the whole of Sunday, and sometimes even over the whole of Saturday, as is the case below the Widdup reservoir of the Halifax Water Works. Throughout this period these foreshores are laid bare, as in a prolonged ebb on a muddy sea-beach. No doubt there had been, under the old *régime*, daily fluctuations in dry weather, as the water was held up or let down by the water-mills above. But these oscillations were small as compared with the holding up of all the water by a gigantic system of impounding reservoirs. Moreover, he had formerly the satisfaction of observing in the decay of those water-mills, and the silting up of their storage dams, some prospect of a great abatement of even these interferences with the natural current.

A grievous injury has been inflicted upon him, as upon every dweller in the vast communities on the banks of the river, and he and they have no redress. Their interest has not been considered. To the law, in effect, it has no existence. But now, on investigating the mystery of this singular change, he realises that all hope is gone; that the waters which, from the days when earth was young—if such days there were—had practically descended in a natural continuous flow, have been decreed by the fiat of a committee to be held up from the river-bed for ever, to be discharged, not for the benefit of the river, with all its diverse and increasing interests, but for the benefit of a very few individuals—sometimes not half-a-dozen—whose interest is yearly decaying. And it is not unknown in the history of compensated rivers, as we shall clearly see hereafter, that these fortunate forestallers and regraters part with this compensation water at a handsome profit. Thus the stream down to a certain point is dried up for ever, and below such point is permanently injured, at the sole cost of all the other interests. Let us now more closely examine and weigh the action and effect of intermittent flow.

Any one who has had to deal with the treatment of foul or turbid water, or with the flow of sewage in tanks or in sewers, knows that continuity of flow, regularity of volume, and coolness of temperature, are important factors in keeping down the undue production of offensive gases. If the flow in a common sewer be continuous and equable, the wetted perimeter is constant, and there is little margin of exposed slime, which under oxidation is a principal cause of stench. There is also no stirring up of the deposit below water level.

But where, as in the case of tidal outfall sewers, there is a daily rise and fall, the production of offensive gases is stimulated; owing, first, to the intermittent exposure of a large surface of the wetted perimeter covered with a new film of putrescent slime; and, second, to the disturbance of that deposit which, during a steady flow, gravitates to the bottom in portions of such sewers.

Similar conditions prevail in the beds of all rivers where agriculture is carried on, and especially in the bed of a river into which sewage or sewer and trade effluents are discharged. Foul water comes in, and foul deposit takes place. This is the case with the Aire, the Calder, the Don, and more or less with all the large streams of the West Riding. They abound with foreshores. Once upon a time these were clean sand and shingle, dividing the pools of clear water in which fish abounded, as they do yet in the Tweed and Yarrow down to the sea. Now these are covered, more or less, with a deposit of black slime in the ordinary state of the stream ; and so, too, are the banks up to the water mark. When this deposit is screened by a sheet of cool water moving equably over it, even if such water be polluted, or when the deposit is quite dry, it is comparatively harmless, the still pools being then the more dangerous producers of the gases of putrefaction. But when alternately covered and exposed for twelve hours of each working day, it is in that condition most influenced by the sun's rays, and most liable to give off noxious vapours.

Further, the swelling of the current by the descent of the compensation water into a stream bed wholly or partly emptied, is equally objectionable. The mud is stirred up, the rank odour exhaled suddenly increases, and without even looking at the current, the observant dweller on the banks of a stream whose natural flow is thus disturbed, can readily detect the swell by his nose alone. It is precisely as if a huge mess of filth had been poured in at no great distance above ; but it is merely the result of the sudden influx of pure compensation water at the stream head, flowing once every twenty-four hours over every square inch of denuded bed. Steam users on such streams, as on the Don at Oughtibridge, well know the effect of these sudden rises from the tail waters of the mills above. They detach and carry away from the banks, boulders, and foreshores, particles of bi-carbonate of iron, commonly called "ochrey" deposit, which peculiarly abounds in the bed of the Don above this point.

By the intermittent system there is a further loss ; that of the cooling effect of a continuous flow. The compensation water is derived from the deep cold springs at the river head, and its withdrawal in dry weather would be exactly paralleled by the withdrawal of every such spring. Who would contend that the withdrawal of all springs for twelve hours each day, is not an injury to any stream?

So much for the daily ebb and flow. On Saturday and Sunday the aberrations of the stream are continuous, entailing, independently of the presence of positive pollution, a distinct sanitary loss. Parks, gardens, and recreation grounds in populous centres are integral parts of public hygiene. Their sites are selected with care, and the land and works are costly to the ratepayers, it being rightly assumed that the community must supply at any reasonable outlay the recreation essential to the body and mind of those who toil under conditions more or less unnatural. In these places people congregate; but, under the present *régime*, they are driven away from the vicinity of our industrial rivers and streams. Every angler knows that if there is a breeze or stream of cool air anywhere on a still, hot, sultry summer's day, it is on the river, which operates like a natural flue by the combined coolness of its waters, and the continuity of its channel. The waterway is a conduit for air as well as water. Hence hygiene demands that, instead of being repelled from the old river-side walks, the public should be attracted to them. Thus the operation of an intermittent compensation which deprives a stream of its natural flow at holiday times, and renders it more unsightly and more insanitary, is in these respects contrary to the public good.

Before closing these remarks on the injury by intermittent flow, a minor branch of the subject demands comment; to wit, the absolute deprivation of certain sections of mountain streams of all compensation whatsoever. The history of water works abounds with examples of this. On the upper feeders of these streams, supply reservoirs are made which are in practice wholly devoted to the uses of the promoters, and give out no direct compensation to the stream; such compensation being discharged from a reservoir lower down. Thus a length of the stream, or streams, corresponding with the distance, or distances, between the compensation reservoir and the supply reservoirs, is practically dried up. Its water is taken over its head, as it were, and it has no compensation. Two arguments are used in defence of this: First, the paramount need of the purer or softer water for trade or domestic use; and, second, the comparative unimportance of those mountain streams to which the total abstraction is confined

In cases where the difference in the relative purity of the water creates a necessity, that plea is unanswerable. The lesser of the two evils must be chosen ; and, undoubtedly, it is a less evil to denude a few miles of beautiful stream of all its best feeders, than to supply water which is not above suspicion. The second argument is less valid, since, however unimportant a stream may be, as the water engineer may find it, it has potentialities to which, as has often been proved in the past, it is not easy to place a limit. It seems, in any case, clearly the duty of a conservancy board not to permit so serious an injury to be wrought merely to save expense to the promoters. It is true that owners, sometimes supinely, but generally from ignorance, or from that subdivision of interest which deprives them of a leader, often neglect to defend these interests in Parliament, and only realise the immense damage inflicted, not only upon the fishing and sporting rights, and the "amenities"of their properties, but also upon their agricultural value, by the substitution in ordinary dry weather of a dry stream bed for their old trout stream. Conservators, therefore, should have power to see justice done to every mile of the river and its feeders.

Sir Francis Powell, M.P., in his petition of this session against the Barnsley Bill, has afforded an example of the value of time in making clear to men's minds how their interests are affected. He deposited no petition last year, but this year he petitioned against the proposal of the Barnsley Corporation to abstract the whole of the waters of the Thickwoods Brook—a strong and pure feeder of the Little Don—with no compensation, except such as was to be delivered miles below his estate. He set forth (Clause 6), " That your petitioner would be entirely deprived of the use and benefit of the waters of the said brook, which are essential for the beneficial enjoyment of his lands on either side of the stream," and that (Clause 10) "*No money payment short of the absolute purchase by the Corporation of the whole of the lands belonging to your petitioner* as aforesaid, whether within or beyond the limits of deviation shown on the deposited plans, would compensate your petitioner for the injury and loss which he would sustain by the carrying out of the proposed works."

The words italicised, though used in a petition against a Private Bill, are not too strong for the occasion. An estate watered by

a beautiful mountain stream is one thing ; the same estate inter-
sected by nothing more than a dry gully is another, and cannot
serve the purposes for which the estate was acquired. Where,
however, the stream is owned by a number of smaller proprietors,
unity is lost, and the strength of an individual case dissipated.
In such a case the central authority, as the defender of the
common interest, should step in.

The Nidd scheme illustrates this phase of the compensation
question. In that scheme, as in its other three separate catch-
grounds, Bradford has adopted the system of separate compensation areas; that is, there is no obligation to discharge a specific
volume of water to the stream impounded, but merely the
obligation to make and maintain a compensation reservoir of a
specific capacity to impound the waters of a specific area for the
sole benefit of the stream below. In carrying out this system,
which is, we believe, unique in the West Riding, some 8 or 10
miles of the River Nidd and the How Stean Beck are destined
to receive no compensation water. The How Stean Beck is the
chief tributary of the Upper Nidd, and is undoubtedly one of the
most remarkable streams in the mountain limestone—a formation
rich in natural curiosities and striking scenes. The Stean flows
for several hundred yards through a vertical chasm in a series
of falls and deep still pools of perfectly clear water, completely
arched and curtained by a luxuriant growth of trees and bushes
and climbing plants. This section is inclosed and laid out as a
pleasure ground, being the principal special attraction of a
singularly beautiful dale. The effect of the total abstraction of
the water only 1½ miles above this little gorge—a gem of
mountain scenery—may be readily imagined.

The preceding analysis of the evil effects of the intermittent
discharge of compensation water suggests, and indeed carries
with it, the arguments for the beneficial effects of an equal and
continuous flow. Whether the volume be one-third or one-fourth
of the total available volume impounded, the river is vastly
improved by the substitution of a regular flow for the variable
dry weather flow yielded by nature. It fills the natural channel
to its normal mean hydraulic depth, shields to a certain extent
that foul deposit which is inevitable, and which can only be
efficiently scoured out by the action of a freshet of at least 30 or

40 times the dry weather flow ; and by its cooling effect further keeps down the evolution of foul gases. What these gases are in hot and dry weather, in a polluted stream, whose mud banks are under process of fermentation, is notorious to those who are familiar with the West Riding, and incredible to those who are not. In a single reach or pool the surface every few minutes is agitated by the "blowing off" of the gas imprisoned at the bottom. It expands and bursts its bonds, carrying up with it the mass of flocculent matter that had weighed upon it. These bubbling eruptions can be heard scores of yards away, and the author has often seen the whole surface of a river literally covered for hundreds of yards with an accumulation of the foul matter so driven upward, the water itself being obscured by it.

It has been claimed for intermittent delivery that the doubled flow of compensation water has a scouring effect for a considerable distance down the stream, and engineers have been found hardy enough to testify to this effect, as in the Barnsley Bill before the Lords' Committee. A single experiment on any compensated stream in the West Riding will effectually dispel this illusion once and for all. When the valves are opened and the streams turned into an empty bed, the momentary effect is to scour it, and the mud, as well as the leaves, sticks, &c., which the wind and gravitation have carried into it during the period of ebb, are floated along for a short distance only. Its velocity and effect soon slacken : at each pool—and every stream is by nature a mere succession of pools and runs—some of the first deposit is dropped, stranded, or carried into an eddy, and a new deposit taken up to meet with a similar fate in some pool below. Light floating matters are thus carried many miles, and the stream does not lose its turbidity until largely reinforced by pure feeders below. Of scour, in the true sense of the word, there is none ; and if there were, what greater injury could there be to a pure stream, than the perennial fouling of its waters by such daily scouring ?

We have tried to make it clear that from a sanitary point of view the intermittent flow of compensation water is a positive and serious injury to any industrial stream. It is also a sanitary injury, though not to an extent so serious, to any agricultural stream. All rivers and streams which in any way are connected with agriculture, the rearing of cattle, &c., are more or less polluted, especially in drought. In every stream horses, sheep, and cattle will stand in the water, strewing the bed with their excrement. Field drains carry in organic matter of every kind, animal and vegetable, from land tilled and grazed. Even the mountain streams become foul during drought to an extent which is incredible to all, save, perhaps, to shepherds and anglers, and the author has seen some of the finest feeders of the Tweed, in a purely pastoral basin, so foul that every stone was coated with the fibrous slime of the wool of sheep from some washing "dub," the pollution increasing daily, until the first "spate" scours it down into the lower reaches of the river itself. Under such circumstances the angler's line gathers slime from the water at each cast. It is thus a mistake, even in the sanitary interest, to contend that purely agricultural streams should be deprived of the natural right to a continuous flow for the benefit of another interest.

III.

RIPARIAN INTERESTS.

Before entering into an attempt to define the full meaning of "riparian interests," some remarks may be addressed to the obvious question, What is the origin of the custom of intermittent flow in England? In England, we say, for it seems to be unknown elsewhere; at any rate it is unknown in Scotland. So far as day and night flow are concerned, there is no distinction across the Border. Hundreds of Acts have been passed there, each enacting a compensation flow for water abstracted, and practically in every case the flow has been continuous. Millowners' interests there do not, or did not in the infancy of compensated streams, greatly differ from the millowners' interests here. They were chiefly those of corn and paper mills, worked by water power, with a few tilt and forge works in certain streams. Neither did the other interests in the streams differ. Why Scotland should originally adopt the natural method, and England the artificial method, and why both should continue two systems exactly opposed to each other in principle, under precisely similar circumstances, is, to say the least of it, a singular example of the power of accident to determine the twist or bent of human policy, unless, indeed, as may well be the case, we attribute it to the superior tenacity of Scotch riparians in holding fast to those rights in running water which are lineally descended from the old Roman law.

Not that we can trace the particular accident—if accident it were—which in England determined that precedent which doubtless paved the way to the general custom of intermittent flow. The records are dumb. The same professional indifference which apparently has ignored the principles governing the use and application of water compensation, has left its origin in mystery. It may be that the history of the " standing orders " of both Houses of Parliament would lend a key to the mystery, but we do not know of the existence of that resource. Smiles, in his "Lives," does not even mention the word compensation in connection with Sir Hugh Myddelton and the New River Water Works, or with Brindley and the canal engineers of the last century ; in fact, the word does not occur in his famous book.

One thing is certain : the custom arose in an age in which conditions widely different from those now around us, prevailed ; an age in which water power was all-important, and that of steam, gas, air, and electricity unknown. That age was probably about the central twenty-five years of the last century; that is, from 1737 to 1762. Probably every available foot of fall in the larger rivers had then been utilized for power. The wants of the people pressed, and every facility was given for putting the force of a moving current of water at the service of man, in substitution of the power of horses and other beasts of burden. The land-owners were then the chief millowners, building their weirs and damming the water, content to suffer injury to their lands from the pent-up current, in order to profit by its power. By degrees they acquired the practical control of the rivers, tempered by lawsuits with their neighbours, as the levels of their weirs grew higher and higher, and threw the land above them more and more into backwater.

Thus when the new system of impounding the higher feeders, first for navigation, and then for town water works, was introduced, the millowners were masters of the situation. Probably they were the sole opponents of the proposed abstraction, and following up what they deemed to be their rights, it was doubtless

e accidental circumstance that an intermittent flow best suited
e majority or their leaders in the first important diversion that
eated the precedent. In the first schemes which followed, the
ecedent probably suited the views of those millowners nearest
e impounding work, their interest being apparently much more
rect, or, at any rate, more manifest, than that of larger mills
wer down, which drew their supply from a wider area ; and so,
the northern counties at least, a custom grew, beneficial to a
ngle interest, and baneful to many others.

What are riparian interests ? That is, the interests in such
owing water as, by its own unaided gravitation, has found its
ay into a defined channel on the earth's surface. We cannot
better than put before our readers the rights of a riparian
vner, as defined by Justice Storey, so far back as 1827 :

" *Prima facie*, every proprietor upon each bank of a river is
ntitled to the land, covered with water, in front of his bank, to
e middle thread of the stream. In virtue of this ownership, he
is a right to the use of the water flowing over it in its natural
rrent, without diminution or obstruction. But, strictly speak-
g, he has no property in the water itself, but a simple use of it
hile it passes along. The consequence of this principle is that
proprietor has a right to use the water to the prejudice of
other. It is wholly immaterial whether the party be above or
low, in the course of the river ; the right being common to all
e proprietors on the river, *no one has a right to diminish the
antity which will, according to its natural current, flow to a
oprietor below*, or to throw it back upon a proprietor above.
his is the necessary result of the perfect equality of right
nongst the proprietors of that which is common to all. The
tural stream existing by the bounty of Providence for the
nefit of the land through which it flows, is an incident annexed,
operation of law, to the land itself. When I speak of this
mmon right, I do not mean to be understood as holding the
octrine that there can be no diminution whatsoever, and no
struction or impediment whatsoever, in the use of the water as
flows, for that would be to deny the valuable use of it. There
ay be, and there must be allowed of that which is common to
l, a reasonable use. The true test of the principle and extent
the use is whether it is to the injury of the other proprietors

or not. . . . The diminution, retardation, or acceleration not possibly and sensibly injurious by diminishing the value of the common right, is an implied element of using the stream at all. But of a thing common by nature there may be an appropriation by general consent or grant. Mere priority of appropriation of running water, without such consent or grant, confers no exclusive right. It is not like the case of mere occupancy, where the first occupant takes by force of the priority of occupancy. That supposes no ownership already existing, and no right to the use already acquired. But our law annexes to the riparian proprietors the right to the use in common as an incident to the land ; and whoever seeks to found an exclusive use must establish a rightful appropriation in some manner known and admitted by the law."

The foregoing definition, though from an American judge, is so complete that Taylor, in his edition of the " Water Works Clauses Acts," says it has been " almost adopted as the text of the law as to the landowners' right to use running water." It is, as we have said, a declaration of the inherited Roman law, set forth in the most clear and comprehensive language, and has been inserted here to enable the reader to appreciate the limitation of the millowners' rights. By millowners are meant in this connection, only the owners, lessees, or occupiers of those mills which work by water power.

But the riparian owners and the millowners, lessees, and occupiers are not the only persons who possess rights in the use and benefit of running waters in the West Riding. There are also the riparian occupiers, the West Riding Rivers Board, the County Council, and each one of these local authorities which have the power of enforcing the Rivers Pollution Act, as well as, in many cases, the navigation companies, who are largely interested, not only in the purity of river water, but also in the continuity of its flow for purposes of traffic.

All these possess rights in their rivers. The rights may vary in extent or value, but the law, it is assumed, protects all rights. As Justice Storey puts it, there is a perfect equality of right, except by special lease or by grant, and it is the object of these remarks to show cause why new rights shall not be created. Yet on consulting the Standing Orders of the two Houses, we find that notices of an application to abstract water from any stream

are to be given, not to all persons interested in such stream, or
to their representatives, but only to the owners, lessees, and
occupiers of all mills, manufactories, or other works using the
water of such streams for a distance of 20 miles below the point
at which such water is intended to be abstracted. The limit of
distance is reasonable, but the limit of interests noticed recognizes
millowners and others using the waters for trade purposes as the
only persons seriously interested in the stream flow. If there
are no such persons, no notice appears to be necessary, and as
we have seen in the case of the Leeds and Liverpool Canal Bill
of 1892, only the vigilance of the County Council prevented an
irreparable injury to the River Aire from almost its source down
to Leeds, owing to the absence of these very millowners. In
practice, however, there is a limit within this limit, for notices
are not usually sent to the owners, &c., of *all* works using the
waters. They are sent to the owners, &c., of mills worked
by water power only, and the vastly greater interests of the other
works are ignored.

The Water Works Clauses Act, 1847, does, indeed, by Clause
12, provide that the undertakers of the works shall make full
compensation to all parties interested for all damage sustained
by them through the exercise of the powers conferred by the
Act. But this right is almost invariably cancelled in effect by
the provision in every Act, of a clause enacting that "the
respective quantities of water allotted to the stream shall be
deemed as full compensation to all persons interested in the flow
of the stream" whose waters are to be abstracted. Thus, in
point of fact, the private act goes behind the common law without
the cognizance of the other interests. As riparians merely they
do not even know that their lawful rights are assailed ; and a
stroke which is unseen cannot be warded off.

Laying aside for the moment the question of the persons
interested, let us now consider what are the interests themselves
served by a stream in its condition as usually found by the
undertakers of a scheme for diverting any part of its waters.
The term "natural" is often conveniently applied to this
condition, though it is obviously incorrect. Perhaps
"unappropriated" would be the fittest term."

A stream, then, in its unappropriated condition serves the

following principal interests, or some of them.

1. Trade including (*a*) water power, (*b*) steam use, and (*c*) trade use for various manufacturing purposes, such as the scouring, dyeing, and washing of wool, and woollen, and other fibre and textile fabrics, paper-making, various branches of metal making, &c.
2. Agriculture.
3. Navigation.
4. Amenities and fisheries.
5. Public health.

Let us analyse these several interests, with the endeavour, if possible, to arrive at some definite idea of their relative importance and the relation of each to the question before us—continuous *versus* intermittent flow.

1. TRADE.

(*a*) *Water Power.*—This interest we take first, not because it is first in importance, but because hitherto it has usually taken precedence in most of the private Acts relating to the abstraction of water from rivers in the north of England. Also, it is the only interest mentioned in the standing order.

Going back to the origin of water mills, it must not be forgotten that every water mill upon a running stream was, in the beginning of mills, an encroachment upon the natural rights of others. At first the encroachment was small, almost infinitesimal where the fall was rapid, the stream being dammed up practically without storage. Originally designed for temporary use only, in the process of time it was found that it would be a convenient thing to run a mill for a longer time in dry weather than the natural current permitted. Then weirs were raised and a little storage got in the stream bed itself. Yet a little more power was wanted, and the discovery was made by some genius that a hole or tank could be made, and the stream above diverted into it, so as to store some part of the night flow for use during the following day. Then by degrees the holes or tanks grew larger, until the state of things came to be what we see it at present ; and, as the appetite grows by what it feeds upon, it has actually been held out as a threat, before a Parliamentary Committee, that if a continuous flow were enacted, the first mill below could, by constructing a reservoir of sufficient capacity, entrap it by night, and so convert it into an intermittent flow. Such an attempt would probably be made, but for one excellent reason, viz., that it is rarely worth while, in these days of railways, cheap coals, and steam, to spend money on new works of water power in this country. Such is the cumulative force of encroachment, whether on rivers or on commons. If the same interference we now behold had been originally attempted as a whole, there is no doubt it would have been resisted.

In dealing, therefore, with the vast majority of water mills, we are dealing with rights which have been gained at the cost and injury of others. This, while not affecting the validity of those rights, has to be considered where their owners come forward, and, with an absolute disregard of all those other interests which they have already injured, make of these rights a basis to claim a new right, and insist that every drop of compensation water intended for the common benefit of all the stream interests, shall be handed over to their sole control.

But even if a prescriptive right to new encroachment were conceded on the ground of asserting the common injury of this single interest, that injury would remain to be proved. It cannot be proved. On the basis of granting one-third the total available yield of any catchground, it is admitted by all competent and impartial authorities that a continuous flow is more beneficial, even to the upper millowners running intermittently, than the stream in its unappropriated state.

What is done by compensation is to give to the stream an equal flow, which on the one hand reduces, and in many cases even does away entirely with, floods and freshets, which do no good and often much harm to mills, displacing their storage capacity with debris, &c. ; and on the other increases the dry weather flow, which also is ineffectual in any case, and is useless without storage. Not only is this the case, but the millowner is master of his work, and on a fairly compensated stream can make his arrangements practically without let or hindrance by the caprices of weather.

The word "compensation" denotes a full *quid pro quó* in the eye of the law. Therefore the river compensation flow must not mean a volume which *on the average only* will. compensate the millowning interest for the water abstracted. Every mill must be left in at least as good a position as before. But so also must every interest, and if this be impossible, then the majority and weight of interests must decide, the minority being compensated by money. There is, however, as a rule, no impossibility.

Where there is no storage, every waterwheel is practically limited in its power to the force of the greatest flow which can be termed regular. Where there is storage sufficient to contain the night flow, the same power is obtained by a wheel working only 12 hours, with only one-half of such regular flow. Such storage dams, however, are extremely rare, and we know of few streams in the West Riding which possess reservoirs holding more than 1 or 1½ hours' storage, even when cleansed of silt, and, as a rule, all dams are more or less silted up, most of them, indeed, to the extent of more than one half their capacity. Further, every such storage dam, no matter how small its use, is, without compensation, a right obtained at the expense of every other interest on the stream. It holds up the water, and while the flow of the river is thus suspended, the riparians below are, for the time being, deprived of the beneficial use of it.

Practically, therefore, it may be laid down that, as a rule, the power of a waterwheel does not exceed the force of the regular flow by more than 10 or 15 per cent., even where regulated by a storage reservoir; and it is found that the ordinary volume granted as compensation by Parliamentary usage—one-third of the total available yield of the catch-ground, will, if delivered in an equal continuous flow, supply a greater force. If proof of this be demanded, we may point to the Scottish millowners, who are more than content with such a flow in such industrial rivers as the Esk, the Leven, and the Carron.

Also, it is a fact that cannot be disputed, that both in Scotland and elsewhere, millowners using their water power intermittently are satisfied with this delivery of the compensation water in an equal continuous flow; and, if this be the case with the higher millowners, much more must it be so with the lower, who, under the intermittent system, have the mortification of knowing that a large part of the compensation water flows past their wheels during the night silently and uselessly, which fact conclusively shows that intermittent flow demands the sacrifice of the rivers, not only to a single interest out of many, but to a section only of that interest.

Now, what is the present position of this interest which, gifted with the power of Aaron's rod, has in too many cases swallowed all other stream interests in the West Riding, to their almost irreparable damage? An American engineer, versed in his 75 or 80 per cent. turbines, and familiar with the hydraulic force of great rivers, regulated by great natural lakes, which is the form almost universally taken by water power in his country, would laugh at the wooden wheels of Old England. These time-honoured and picturesque structures, however suited to the pencil of a David Cox, can, as a rule, especially in the centre of a coalfield, lay no claim to that beauty of utility which consists in a perfect adaptation of the means to the end so as to secure the best scientific result. How, then, do matters stand with this relic of antiquity—water power?

The answer is, that in every river in the West Riding, as on rivers of all districts in which coal is cheap, water power is rapidly declining in use and value. Let us take the River Don. In 1874, when the old Wakefield Water Company were applying to Parliament for their Langsett scheme on the Little Don, schedules were presented to the Lord's Committee, setting forth the name, owner, fall, power, and working hours of every watermill within 20 miles from the proposed impounding reservoir. Last year, after the lapse of 21 years only—a brief span in the history of an industry—the effective power of these mills had decreased by one-third. There were, in 1874, 30 mills; now there are 20, while of the remainder a large number of the wheels have been taken out, or are useless from decay. Of the 10 that are gone four have been entirely demolished; three burnt down, the last about nine years ago; one is a heap of ruins; and the other two disused for over 10 years, and in a ruinous state of decay, the wheels rotten, and the mill-race filled up. The vast majority of the wheels still working are of an obsolete antiquated type—mostly, in fact, the old radial paddle, low-breasted, or "four o'clock" wheels, yielding, when in good condition, about 30 per cent. of duty, but mostly in poor repair. There are but three or four turbines in all, and scarcely a new wheel of any kind has been put in throughout the 20 years. Even in 1874, the total duty derived from this length of the river, down to the old Brightside corn mill, below Sheffield, was estimated at 1100 to 1200 H.P. ; at the present moment it is not 800 H.P. ; while it was given in evidence, in the Barnsley Bill, that at one single concern alone, the Stocksbridge Iron Works, the steam power was 13,000 H.P., or 16 times as much! Yet the owners of this vast steam user's interest get no notice, as steam users, and have no power.

Below Sheffield, the water power is still more insignificant. There are but nine small mills, two of which have been in ruins for years ; and it is significant that for the sole benefit of one of these ruined mills—Kilnhurst Forge—a special compensation was granted by the Doncaster Water Works Act of 1873 ; and that this, an equal continuous flow, is now being delivered for the benefit of the polluted Don without let or hindrance, the forge being in ruins. Thus time and the decay of the water power have in this case yielded a natural solution of the stock difficulty so regularly raised by the opponents of continuous flow, viz., that the storage dam of each mill converts it to an intermittent flow.

We see, then, something of the true nature and proportion of the water power interest. On the whole of the main stream of the Don it is probably not one-twelfth part of the power interest in the single great steam works we have cited. So it is elsewhere. On the Calder, the Aire, and even the Nidd, which formerly was far more of an industrial river than the Wharfe, and where coal is more distant and costly, the same story is told. If a watermill be burnt down, it is unprofitable to rebuild it, and in three cases out of four it is not rebuilt. There in the river bed is the force of the regular current, there is the millowner's prescriptive right ; these remain, but the profitable user is gone, owing to the change wrought by a cheaper and more constant motor. Where coal is cheap and abundant, the force of the water in these precarious streams, like that of the wind or tide, is treated with contempt, and no one dreams of putting up a new watermill for industrial purposes.

Here we may fitly deal with, and if possible dispose of, the objection above cited, namely, that continuity of flow cannot be secured so long as the existing mills and other storage dams remain. True, but as a millowner shrewdly said in cross-examination, "Every millowner would object to a new mill and dam to hold up the water, and here you propose a dam as big as all the rest put together, to hold the water over our heads." What is done is done, and the right remains. In this world counsels of perfection are generally time lost, and we must do what good we can, not what we wish. This contention of the opponents of continuous flow is, we freely admit, the strongest they can advance, and we desire to meet it fairly. As has been stated, few mills have more than 1 to $1\frac{1}{2}$ hour's storage of that regular flow required for useful effect, even when at their full capacity, and this is mostly reduced by silting to one-half. Large mills have often but a few minutes' storage ; and we are satisfied that the whole of the reserves of the watermills on such rivers as the Don, Calder, and Aire, will not, under their usual conditions, contain the total night flow of the compensation water, *plus* the natural or direct flow from the non-appropriated districts extending for a distance of at least a dozen miles, respectively from each of the several impounding works. If this be so, although continuity is not secured, yet a great step in that direction is taken. The period of dilution of the normal continuous flow of sewage is increased ; the period of ebb and exposure of stinking banks and foreshores is decreased ; and though the night flow descends step by step, halting at each step to charge a tank or reserve pool, at each step it does good, reinforcing and renovating the polluted current.

Further, the inevitable march of decay goes on with accelerated steps ; this gives hope. Practically, water power on these little rivers, whose banks are a continuous hive of workers, is doomed ; and it is certain that each decade will see the mills decrease, and the halts of the obstructed current become fewer, until the time is ripe for that step which enthusiasts may deem probable, and which the author thinks possible—the purchase of the relics of the old water power, at any rate so far as the impounding works are concerned. Such an undertaking would help to complete the work of restitution, and it seems only just that the private adventurers who committed the outrage—not that of the original interference, but that of the new-fangled intermittent flow—should see their own interests decay until their value in fee simple will add no great burden to the rateable value of 7 millions sterling. But the bare possibility of this should redouble the efforts of the Rivers Board to secure a continuous flow. Clearly, intermittent flow for the benefit of a few individuals is a new right, and a wise legislation will shut the door for ever against the creation of a new right in running water.

(b) *Steam Use.*—We have touched upon the question of steam use incidentally in dealing with the water power interest. A moment's consideration suffices to show the vast, almost infinite disproportion in value between them. While water power on the West Riding rivers is reckoned by hundreds, steam power is reckoned by scores of thousands; steam power, that is, serving riparian interests only. The import of this lies in the fact that all highly polluted waters, and especially where that pollution is strongly impregnated with acid, are costly and dangerous to boilers. The effects are twofold : first, the acids corrode the metal ; and, second, the sedimentary pollutions cause deposit, hinder the generation of steam, and increase the danger of explosion. That these rivers largely contain acids is well known. In the woollen districts the dyeing processes consume much acid. In the iron districts about Sheffield, in Halifax, and in other towns, diluted muriatic acid, a most corrosive liquid, is largely discharged from the wire-drawing works, and has a destructive effect on boilers. In their petition against the Dewsbury and Barnsley Bills, the Sheffield steam users laid special emphasis on the fact of these acid pollutions, alleging the pernicious effect of withdrawing any portion of the clear water. Moreover, the volume of ochrey water discharged by the coal and ironstone mines on the Upper Don and its feeders is, as has been already been said, continuous. The bicarbonate of iron it contains permanently discolours the current, and has a most corrosive effect upon the boilers. In his evidence against the Barnsley Bill last year, Mr. J. D. Ellis, chairman of Sir John Brown and Co., stated that they were unable to use the Don water for many of their boilers by reason of its fouling. Under the new Sheffield Act, all the chief ochrey feeders in the catch-ground will in future be diverted into a single channel, and discharged at a single point into the Little Don. If the discharge of this noxious water be continuous, as it must be, so also should be that of the pure compensation water which is so necessary for dilution. The temporary drying up of the stream concentrates both the acids and the pollutions; whereas, on the contrary, the continuous flow of fresh water dilutes both. The doubled flow for 12 hours is not a benefit, but the reverse so far as the sediment is concerned, and of course is no more utilised down the river by the steam users than by the millowners. Sheffield is an instance of this. When the Ewden appropriated area, the stream from which will be intermittently compensated, is in use, the bulk of the compensation water will pass through Sheffield after midday.

(c) *Trade Use.*—What applies to steam use applies still more forcibly to many branches of trade use, as, for instance, the scouring, dyeing, and washing of wool and other fibres, yarns, and fabrics, and papermaking. The volumes of river water used for this purpose are immense, it being no uncommon thing for a single firm of woollen manufacturers or paper makers to use half a million gallons of river water daily. Again, the great iron and steel industries in Sheffield use still more, and although purity is not so important here, yet from a sanitary point of view it is more so. An extract from a Sheffield evidence against the Barnsley Bill in the Lord's Committee last year was conclusive on this point.

Mr. J. Utley said that during the recent visit of the Duke of York, the royal visitors went over the great works of Charles Cammell and Co., but they were not asked to witness the process of hardening steel plates because of the tremendous amount of noxious water that would have to be used, which they thought would not be safe. If not safe for great personages, it cannot be safe for the humble workers themselves. There can be no doubt that the negative pollution due to the prolonged abstraction of compensation water under the intermittent, system, is one great cause of this intense foulness in dry weather. Once more the continuous flow of pollution into a stream carries with it the absolute necessity of a continuous flow of pure water to balance the abstraction.

Other trades there are in plenty, all having an interest in the natural flow of running water, as, for instance, tanning, fellmonging, brewing, malting, &c. ; but enough has been said to show the absolute insignificance of the water power interest —and that of the upper sections of the rivers only—as compared with the innumerable other trade interests which are yearly waxing bigger and bigger as the former grows less. We now come to

2. AGRICULTURE.

It is obvious that agriculture is, and ever will be, largely interested in running water. At no single point is that interest so concentrated and valuable as that of great manufacturers and others in towns, but its interest is practically continuous, beginning at the source, and ending only at the open sea. And if the interest of the lowland section of a stream in any one out of a score of strong feeders is comparatively small, yet that interest enters into the whole of them, and in every case is prejudiced by the adoption of a principle which, when applied to most of the best feeders, will by degrees render any stream practically stagnant water for the best part of its existence.

The agricultural uses of a river are chiefly :

(*a*)   As a boundary or fence.

(*b*)   As a means of watering cattle.

(*c*)   For irrigation and warping lowlands.

(*a*)   *Boundary.*—In its natural state a river is a boundary, being generally a division not only between tenants, but also between owners. By the intermittent flow this use is prevented in the upper sections of a stream. A very moderate current suffices to prevent cattle from straying across a stream, and though the minimum flow usually will not, such minimum flow is of rare occurrence, and can, to some extent, be guarded against. Nothing short of a new fence can, as a rule, effectually protect a boundary stream which is emptied of its principal water once a day. When we come to the question of

(*b*)   *Watering Cattle,* we find that although the river may still be a fence in its lower reaches, yet its pollutions, heightened as they are by the intermittent flow of compensation water, often render it necessary to fence it off on both sides, to prevent cattle from straying, not across, but into, the river and drinking its poisonous water. At a meeting of the West Riding River

Board, held on March 20th, 1896, the chairman emphasised the importance of two letters complaining of the pollution of a brook at Swallow Nest, in the Doncaster rural district. One of these was from a farmer, who stated that during the past eighteen months he had lost cattle and horses to the value of £200, through their drinking water from the running stream upon which every field in his farm abutted. The veterinary surgeon who attended the animals informed him that there was no other cause of death, and that once the water got into their systems there was no remedy. The chairman stated that he understood that the poisonous effect was constantly occurring in the West Riding. That this is so is an undoubted fact.

The injury accruing to human beings from eating the flesh of cattle fed on the banks of such streams, which cattle, though not poisoned outright, are killed before the water has produced its full effect, cannot be estimated. We violate nature in one principle, and we think we may escape her avenging hand ; nevertheless she exacts the full penalty. We poison our flood at its source, and shudder at the spread of cancer and other mysterious complaints. The positive pollution is the basis of the injury, but undoubtedly the negative pollution of denying to the river the fullest dilution of its poisonous affluents, makes its effect more deadly.

(c) *Irrigation and Warping.*—Water irrigation is by no means common in the West Riding, and no great stress need be laid upon it ; while warping, which is the admission of large and continuous volumes of river water, heavily charged with rich sediment, on to the surface of low-lying lands, in order that such sediment may be deposited to the depth of 3 ft. or more, is only carried on where the river water, though not salt, is within reach of tidal influence. Still, while not relatively of great importance, continuity of flow is a benefit to both interests.

3. NAVIGATION.

This is a great interest ; it comes next in degree in point of commercial value to that of agriculture. It is an interest which essentially demands a continuous flow—a flow as nearly equalised as possible.

The nearer uniformity of level can be secured in a canalised stream—for that is the sense in which the term "navigable" is here used—the better the traffic can be worked both up-stream and down-stream, such level being the normal level fitted to the draught of boats. Even a few inches in the height of a weir is often of the utmost importance, and a dispute on this small difference in the level of lock and weir sills has led to costly litigation. Almost every stream in the Riding is a feeder to a canalised river, but owing to the singular fact that the standing order limit of all special notices of intention to divert water ends at the confluence with the first navigable stream, it has been often assumed in practice that the owners of a navigation have no interest to be compensated.

Also, from a sanitary standpoint, all the West Riding navigations are interested in continuity of flow, the state of the rivers often becoming so bad in years of drought that the effluvium is a direct cause of disease and death to boatmen and others, as well as a hindrance to traffic. As an extreme instance of this, the case of the Bradford Canal may be cited. Owing to the intensity of its pollution, the canal was unworkable for a considerable period, and its use could only be continued by abandoning its original source of supply, the Bradford Beck. This—probably in its day the paramount nuisance of the West Riding—has been remedied ; but the Aire and Calder and the Calder and Hebble Navigations, still exist. Of the former, Mr. W. H. Bartholomew, M. Inst., C.E., who had then been forty years engineer and general manager, said in 1894, before the Commons Committee on the West Riding Rivers Bill, that these rivers were practically filthy sewers ; and, despite all the improvements of science and the jealous control of the Rivers Board, they must remain foul rivers until the trade and population of this great Riding have passed away.

4. Amenities and Fishing.

These may be termed the minor interests of the rivers of the Riding, although on the upland feeders of some rivers they are the paramount interest. The value of an estate is enhanced by its beauty, to injure which is to injure the value of the estate. Nor can it be denied that a fine stream is an element of beauty, nor that to dry it up, or to materially lower its current twelve hours every day, and from Saturday afternoon to Monday, is an injury to its beauty. Sir Francis Powell's petition, already cited, shows the light in which the total loss of the stream is regarded. Nothing short of the purchase of the whole estate can compensate that, and a total loss on the best days in the week does not demand much less.

The fishing interest is obvious. It may be slighted by money-makers who wish to see more smoke in their district, and who, when their race is run, can say, "I have amassed a fortune ; I have destroyed a stream. *Nunc dimittis.*" But it is often, when combined with the scenery, the principal attraction of a large and valuable property. To this interest also a continuous flow is an absolute necessity for spawning and other purposes. The habits of fish, and especially of the trout and the salmon, are such that anything like the total abstraction of water in a river bed, even for the twelve hours of an intermittent flow, is fatal to the spawn lying on the clean beds of gravel, one essential condition of their vitality being a constant screen or covering of pure running water. Below the pure feeders this injury does not happen, for the sporting fish do not spawn there ; but in streams moderately polluted, dilution is a necessary of life to the fish in their lower sections.

5. PUBLIC HEALTH,

This, the last of the great interests in running waters, has been already described to some extent. Though not originally a legal right, it has been made so since the passing of the Rivers Pollution Prevention Act of 1876. Until that time the public, no matter how largely they suffered from the state of a river, had no direct means of redress, not being recognised by the law either as to damage by positive pollution, or by negative pollution of its waters ; and even under that Act, the right is practically inoperative. For all practical purposes in the West Riding, the right has only existed for two years, or since the passing of the West Riding Rivers Act in 1894. That Act recognized that public health demands the free carriage of all the matters, liquid or solid, which must enter the stream, whether from natural or artificial sources, the current at the same time being unobstructed by the undue aggregation of solids, and unpolluted beyond a certain practical degree.

It is self-evident that all refuse matters must directly or indirectly enter the river. Even if they are burnt, the vapours cannot altogether waste in the air. The rain and dews precipitate aerial pollution, visible and invisible, and they too must gravitate by pollution and otherwise to the running waters. Within the limited area of the West Riding there is a population of $2\frac{1}{2}$ millions, or three human beings to every two acres. From this enormous hive, making woollens and other necessaries for the whole country, and for a goodly share of the world besides, every particle of refuse must find its way to the streams, more or less purified. The manurial lands must drain there, the sewage must drain there, the trade effluents must drain there, the beasts and cattle must drain there, and the crowded cemeteries, churchyards, and other burial grounds must also drain there. When science has reached its *ne plus ultra* in the purification of the rivers, still the running water will need all the dilution it can get of the impurities which must enter.

It is this fact which destroys the argument that, once the river is purified, a duty which, of course, devolves upon the Rivers Board, the sanitary need of a continuous flow will cease to exist. There never will be a time in which the West Riding rivers will have become so pure that an intermittent flow will have ceased to be a source of danger to public health, so long as there is a public.

The foregoing assessment of the various riparian interests, may be thought practically complete, and enough has been said to enable some kind of comparison to be shown as to their relative value.

On the one side is the water power interest, which is decreasing yearly, and which, no matter what its assumptions have been in the past, is the least of all the chief riparian interests here dealt with. On the other side are ranged the vast trade interests, including that of the steam users and the water users, which are immense, and are yearly increasing ; the agricultural interest, of which unhappily the same cannot at present be said, but which, for that very reason, demands relief from the checks and hindrances of poisonous streams ; navigation, amenities, and fisheries ; and, finally, public health. These are great odds.

But, fortunately, the millowners have learnt the old lesson that it is lawful to learn from the enemy, and have themselves increased the odds. It is now but the upper section of the millowners, and, moreover, even of them, only those who work intermittently, who demand an intermittent discharge of compensation water. The rest, where they have looked carefully into the question at all, no longer regard the promoters of a continuous flow as enemies, but as friends. Without presumption, therefore, we may regard the contest between the several promoters of the two methods of discharge as too unequal to last much longer; and it will not be surprising if the capitulation of the Sheffield millowners puts an end to it; or at least to anything further than a paper opposition to the just requirements of the Rivers Board. But in any case the small and transitory interest, which is divided, must give way to the great and united permanent interests in an equal continuous flow. Thus natural rights, like healthy seeds, buried in the loam of ages, contain the principle of life, and only need the light in order to fructify once more.

IV.

THE CONTROL OF WEST RIDING RIVERS.

THE second question in connection with compensation water is, who shall control it? Its use or abuse has a grave influence on weighty interests; these, therefore, must strive to lodge the power where it is least likely to be abused. Of course the law enacts a control in each case. As a condition inseparable from their privilege of diverting water for their own uses, the undertakers are bound under penalties to discharge the compensation water in the respective volumes and at the respective times specified. But who is to enforce the law? Much depends upon that, as the past history of river compensation proves. Who is to say that the undertakers' gauges are right, and that they are rightly used and efficiently maintained; and, if they are not, who is to recover the penalties? In short, what authority shall be trusted to secure administration of the law with an equal regard to all the interests, and to control the negative pollution of rivers? the first being the explicit, and the second the implicit, meaning of this important function.

With the existence of a Rivers Board there should be but one answer to this question. An authority which has been specially called into existence to arrest the extremity of the positive pollution, and to restore the rivers of the Riding from a condition disgraceful to civilisation, should logically have the power to arrest their negative pollution. No logical reason can be given for divorcing these duties ; the one is the complement of the other, and the two form the whole duty of a conservancy board in respect of rivers pollution. Sir James Kitson's committee says the two shall be divorced, and that not only shall we exclude the Rivers Board—the common representative of all the riparian interests—but also every other single interest, save one. The millowners, and they only, shall have power to enforce penalties. " True," the committee say in effect, " the millowners grudge " every gallon of water sent down past their mills on Sunday ; but " they, and they only amongst all the interests, shall see that the " exact legal Sunday flow shall be sent down ; and if they choose " not to do so, we will take care that no other power shall do it " —the law shall remain an empty voice, and nothing else. " And, if the undertakers choose to acquire all the water mills " on any compensated stream, as other promoters have done " before them, they shall be at liberty to divert every drop of the " compensation flow, without being liable to any penalties except " such as they themselves shall enforce against themselves." This remarkable decision is given in the face of unquestioned evidence of gross abuse of the millowners' powers on other streams.

Here then, is a single interest out of many interests affected by the interference of persons outside, with the economy of a stream. The natural conditions being thus interfered with, by the impounding and diversion of any part of its waters, it follows that all the interests below the point of interference possess an " equality of right," as Justice Storey puts it, to compensation. Each interest is prejudiced, and, therefore, each has its claim. For the due protection of all the claims in respect of that which is common to all, each interest is entitled to fair representation. If joint representation be unwieldy or impracticable, and an interest exist representative of all the interests, obviously it will be just, convenient, and business-like to give the power of enforcing the law to that interest for the common protection of the whole, at the same time giving each person interested the right to inspect the gauges. This appears to be the only conclusion that an impartial judgment can arrive at after a full consideration of the question ; to reject which, and to put the power into the hands of the only interest which, as a body, will derive a direct benefit from the violation of the law, seems an anomaly in the administration of justice.

In dealing with things human, we must reckon with human nature and its infirmities. Even the individual has his weaknesses, and corporate bodies are universally said to multiply them. A river, let us assume, has its Sunday compensation. The millowners grudge it, and the undertakers of the water works are indifferent. But a time comes when they are no longer indifferent—a time of drought. They covet the Sunday compensation, not for the river, which, indeed, may flow in another valley, but for themselves. The water is worth say, 4d. per thousand gallons to them, while to the only persons who can sue for penalties, it is worth nothing. If a bargain be struck, and the Sunday flow be sold by the millowners to the undertakers, who is to complain, and what becomes of the equality of right amongst all the riparian interests ? A Parliamentary Committee has *de facto* altered the time-honoured law, and thus decreed that there shall no longer be equality of right. There is no representative control, and every other interest finds its mouth closed, and must be content to suffer dumbly the injustice which it experiences.

Further, even the week-day compensation may be sold. A million gallons a day at 4d. per thousand gallons would be worth 16l. 13s. 4d. for town supply. To an ordinary mill with, say, 12 ft. fall, such a volume would yield with the very best wheel that can be devised, about 4½ horse power for about 12 hours. But the average wheels of the West Riding will certainly not yield more than two-thirds of this power, or, say, 3 horse-power per day of 12 hours, worth, as compared with the coal, oil, &c., necessary for obtaining the same result by steam, a few shillings only—not even the odd 3s. 4d.

It may readily be conceived that under the circumstances, and inspired by a purely benevolent desire to relieve the extremity of a water famine, a body of millowners might profitably barter away any portion of the compensation due to the stream ; and, if it be argued that such things would not be done in practice, we may be permitted to recall a few episodes in the history of compensated streams.

In 1887, the Heywood Water Works company obtained powers to purchase about three-sevenths of the compensation water authorised by their Act of 1855 to be sent down for the benefit of the millowners on the Naden Brook, on which the water was not only used for power, but for the vastly more important purposes of washing, scouring, fulling, and milling of flannel and other woollen fabrics. Here the great bulk of the catchground was practically appropriated for town supply, and the stream denuded in perpetuity. The clause in the Act authorising this purchase gave the money compensation for the reduction in the compensation water to "the owners and occupiers for the time being of the mills in the Naden Brook entitled to the use and benefit" of the said compensation water, and to no others. All other interests were ignored.

In 1854, the Manchester Corporation obtained powers to purchase, by agreement, $4\frac{1}{2}$ millions of gallons daily, being about one-third of the total compensation water sent down from their old works, for the use and benefit of the millowners on the River Etherow. This huge volume realised 49,450l., which sum was divided by the owners of seven mills, mostly print works, who thus at one and the same time made money out of both the positive and the negative pollution of what originally was a beautiful mountain stream ; first, by pouring filth into it, and secondly, by keeping pure water out of it. The storage works for this volume had cost the corporation at least 200,000l., and new works to supply the same volume could not have been executed on the residue of the catchground for less than double that amount.

In both these cases Parliament authorised the sale of the water ; but the compensation for that which, by the law, was common to all the interests, accrued to the millowners only, almost the whole of whom had, by their polluting effluents, damaged all other interests. Thus by a private Act the natural and legal equality of other rights was destroyed. In other cases millowners have appropriated the compensation water due to the stream without Parliamentary sanction.

In the year 1893 the Don millowners sold to the Joint Water Works Board of Dewsbury and Heckmondwike a certain portion of the water which, under their Acts, that Board were bound to discharge into the Don as full compensation for diverted waters to all the interests in the stream. The volume sold was 83,500,000 gallons, and the purchase money 2556*l*., which went into the millowners' pockets. Evidence to this effect was given during the hearing of the Barnsley Bill in Parliament last session ; and the witness, who was the borough surveyor of that town, lauded the kind and public-spirited way in which the millowners had met the wants of Barnsley, who procured this auxiliary supply through the medium of the Dewsbury and Heckmondwike Joint Water Works Board.

No doubt the assistance thus rendered in time of need was of material benefit to humanity ; but in plain English both the millowners and the Board, and their Barnsley customers, who sold it to the manufacturers, made a handsome profit out of a commodity which belonged in equity to all the interests in the stream, although by the Act it was supplied solely for the use of the millowners and of the River Don Navigation. This kind of public spirit, which generously applies the property of Peter to pay Paul, has existed as long as the human race, and will only die out with it. This very year has witnessed similar appropriations ; such as at Heywood, whose compensation to the Naden Beck already mentioned as having been reduced by these-sevenths in 1887, was further reduced in August last by one million gallons daily, with a £50 penalty for such days.

Cases could be cited which go farther even than the above to illustrate the arbitrary method in which streams in the West Riding, where the water power is of such insignificant relative value, have been taken possession of by the millowners to the exclusion of every other interest ; cases such as that already mentioned as having been given in evidence before Sir James Kitson's committee, namely, the purchase of all the water power on a minor stream, and the summary diversion of every drop of the statutory compensation ; regardless not only of all the other interests of the stream, but also of the interests of every millowner in the river into which the stream discharges.

Again, it is but a few years ago that the inveterate spirit of stream monopoly culminated at Silsden, a few miles above Bradford, in the Aire Valley. The Bradford compensation reservoir sent down a continuous flow for the benefit of the mills, dye-houses, and other works, and of the Aire and Calder Navigation. A tank was made by the local authority just below the compensation gauge, which impounded a part of the flow for conversion into town sewage. Thus the continuous flow was partly converted into an intermittent flow, as has often been threatened. No legal grant to do this appears to have been acquired, and the transaction is an admirable illustration of the view taken by individuals of the equality of right in running water. At present the daily consumption from this tank does not seriously affect the volume of compensation sent to the stream, but increase of population may swallow the whole of it ; while as the pure water decreases the sewage increases. This is a precedent which might be carried to further extent elsewhere. There are also cases in which certain of the millowners themselves impeach their own administration, the lower millowners alleging that one or two upper millowners can, and practically do, control the water as their own interest directs, without any regard to that of the rest, setting at defiance every regulation as to procedure laid down by the Act in virtue of which they exercise power. In fact, it may be taken as an axiom that the injury inflicted by the upper millowner upon the lower has hitherto been limited by his power only.

These are a few facts in the history of rivers under the control of a single interest. Let us now contemplate the prospects of a very different *regime*, not, we trust, distant in the future.

From the past, we can augur the future ; and we may profitably trace the gradual reintroduction of that fundamental principle of equality of right, which, in the history of West Riding streams, has been far more honoured in the breach than in the observance.

To begin with, it may be premised that the recognition of certain rights, other than those of millowners, has doubtless been coeval with the introduction of Acts for the diversion of water. But these, down to a recent time, have, in most cases in the West Riding, been special rights, mostly acquired by Parliamentary power.

For instance, in the Stockton and Middlesbrough Corporation Water Works Act of 1876, there were associated with the millowners and occupiers, three other interests, viz., the Corporation of Darlington, the Tees Conservancy Commissioners, and the Tees Salmon Fisheries Board; the four interests constituting a Board of control regulating the discharge of the compensation water. Here an equal continuous flow was enacted in the interest of three out of the four controlling authorities, it being clearly seen that it would not do to intrust the carrying out of this principle to the millowners alone. A joint board of this kind is far more cumbersome than that of a single representative body.

In 1882, the Todmorden Water Works Act was passed, also enacting a "regular and continuous flow" of compensation water. In this case, failure to send the proper volume entailed a separate liability to each mill occupier; to the proprietors of the Calder and Hebble Navigation; and to the undertakers of the Aire and Calder Navigation. Here, again, it was decided that the millowners could not be trusted; but it is to be remarked that although the Act provided that the compensation water should be accepted by "the parties interested" as full compensation for the diverted water, the rights of all other riparians to recover damages were ignored.

In both these cases, and in many others similar, the joint control was given to special interests having already, no doubt, Parliamentary powers over the streams affected. But going back a long way, we find, in 1854, a remarkable exception, which might cause a philosophic mind to doubt the progress of riparian ethics. In that year the Bradford Water Works Company got an Act providing that a certain compensation, in an "equal, constant, and continuous flow," should be discharged from and out of the Silsden Reservoir for the supply of mills and other works, and for the Aire and Calder Navigation; and that if the company made default of discharging such compensation they should pay 5l. for each day of such default to each occupier of the mills worked by water power, and to each occupier of the *dye-houses or dye-works* on the Silsden Beck and the River Aire, who might sue for and recover the same, and also 10*l*. to the Aire and Calder Navigation. The gauge was to be open to the inspection of the " owners, lessees, and occupiers *of the present and future mills and works interested,*" and of the undertakers of the said Navigation. Thus, so far back as 42 years ago, other purely trade interests than those of water mill owners made good their equality of right before Parliament, with this limit, that although the owners, lessees, and occupiers of all future mills and works had a right to inspect the gauge, no right was given to the occupiers of future dye-works to recover damages. But the equality exists on paper only, for this is the very compensation flow which, as we have already related, is now converted by an intercepting tank from a continuous into an intermittent flow, and that by a corporate body previously possessing no riparian interests ! Slow indeed is the gathering up of the lost threads of justice.

In the last-mentioned case the right of a second trade interest was recognised. We next come—at a long interval—to the recognition of the right of an ordinary riparian—a landowner pure and simple. In 1888, the Halifax Corporation Water Works Act provided for a continuous flow on the petition of Sir John Savile, as already related ; and, as a matter of course, it was enacted that the compensation gauge or gauges should be " made and maintained to the satisfaction of him and his successors, of the owners and occupiers of the present and future mills and works on the said streams and rivers, and of *all other persons interested in the water so to flow.*" Further, Sir John Savile and the millowners were empowered to repair the gauges if the corporation failed to do so ; but—and here once more came the inevitable failure of perfect equality of right—the only persons to receive compensation for damages by reason of the default of the corporation in discharging the water, were Sir John Savile and the occupiers of the mills and works. This seems to be the earliest instance in which in any degree the rights of all the persons possessing an interest in running waters have been distinctly recognised in a West Riding Water Works Act.

With the advent of the county council a great step towards the integration of the varied interests in rivers is marked. In 1890, the Bradford Corporation Water Works Act called into

existence a river board of management consisting of the millowners on the River Nidd ; three riparians on the river to be
appointed by the West Riding County Council; two persons to
be appointed by the Corporation of York ; two persons to be
appointed by the York New Water Works Company ; and two
persons to be appointed by the Knaresborough Improvement
Commissioners, as the water authority of that town, using the
river as its source of supply. This board is called the Gouthwaite
Board of Management, Gouthwaite being the name of the
compensation area and reservoir devoted to the river. There
was no West Riding Rivers Board in existence then ; hence
representatives of the various water-supplying authorities were
necessary on the board to guard against undue pollution from
any cause, as well as against default in discharging the required
volume.

In the Morley Water Works Act, 1890, no River Board was
instituted, owing to the almost complete appropriation of the
head waters of the Calder by other water authorities and by
navigation, nor was the county council represented directly or
indirectly. The gauge and other works were to be open to the
inspection of the undertakers of the Aire and Calder and Calder
and Hebble Navigations respectively, and also of the occupiers
of all mills *and works interested.* and these interests had the
power of enforcing repairs and penalties. It was doubtless
considered that in this case the control of the continuous flow
was safe in the hands of the navigation companies, whose
interests, as we have seen, demand it.

By the Leeds and Liverpool Canal Act, 1892, the power of
inspecting the true River Aire compensation gauges, and of
repairing them in default of the company's doing so, was put
into the hands of the county council and the corporations of
Leeds and Keighley, but the corporations only are entitled to
damages in default of the proper discharge, the Act making no
mention of any other interest in relation to the River Aire compensation, as distinct from the Winterburn Beck compensation,
which, as has already been explained, was an illusory compensation only, poured into the beck at one point, to be taken out
at another, and diverted into the canal.

Thus we find the curious anomaly that, prior to the existence of the West Riding Rivers Board, every Act providing for a continuous flow at the instance of the County Council also provided that they should have some share in the control ; whereas, in the very first Act providing for such flow since the constitution of the Rivers Board—the Sheffield Water Works Act, 1896—they have been refused any share in the control, although the enactment of a continuous flow, finally agreed to by the millowners, was owing solely to their intervention.

This kind of Private Bill legislation is not progress. It is a grave reflection upon such legislation, and it may well be considered whether the power of allotting the control should be left within the discretionary power of any committee where a Rivers Board exists. Such a board should, it seems clear, possess the sole power of recovering penalties, the common law, by direct parliamentary statute, giving the right of inspection to all the other interests in the stream, and also the power of suing for and recovering damages for default proven ; thus putting it beyond the power of three or four private members, or a majority of them, to destroy equality of right, and to perpetuate that chaos which presides over the destiny of rivers. This involves no more than a fixed principle in English law. A man is fined for furious driving, and remains still liable to compensate all persons damaged by such driving—so much to the county for a breach of the law ; and so much to the party whose person or property is injured.

The author's task is done. He has endeavoured to act as the fair exponent of a question which, though obscure, is undeniably of great importance, and whose obscurity renders exposition · imperative. The recent history of compensation flow in the West Riding ; the significance of a continuous flow as compared with an intermittent flow ; an analysis of those interest in running water commonly called riparian interests ; and, finally, some account of what may be called the fight for the gauges ; these have been placed before those who are interested in the question. It appears clear that the public good, which includes the ends of justice, can in the long run only be secured by placing the whole economy of our rivers, whether in the West Riding or out of it, in the hands of single authorities, which shall be at once representative, powerful, and independent, each working in its own convenient watershed, and not interfering with the right of outside authorities to divert water for public use under the safeguards we have sketched. In this way only can all the interests in running waters be integrated against the forces of malappropriation.

The question of intermittent flow *versus* continuous flow is now almost solved in the West Riding. In the last struggle the enemy themselves—the millowners—have been brought over. Like all fair opponents, they have themselves helped to sift the truth by questioning it, thus throwing the burden of proof on to the reformers ; and a truth realised by slow degrees and by the cumulative weight of evidence, is more valued than one taken for granted. Every such conflict teaches us Bacon's lesson that we can only command nature by obeying her. But this applies to the West Riding only. Others have the lesson to learn ; and one main object in essaying this slight treatise on the subject is to induce the rest of the county and river authorities throughout the country to come into line with the West Riding County Council on this important phase of rivers conservancy—the negative pollution of running waters.

ELLAND : PRINTED BY HENRY WATSON.

www.ingramcontent.com/pod-product-compliance
Lightning Source LLC
Chambersburg PA
CBHW031800090426
42739CB00008B/1100